Twelve Beds for the Dreamer

TWELVE BEDS FOR THE DREAMER

Máighréad Medbh

TWELVE BEDS FOR THE DREAMER

is published in 2011 by
ARLEN HOUSE
an imprint of Arlen Publications Ltd
42 Grange Abbey Road
Baldoyle
Dublin 13
Ireland
Phone/Fax: 353 86 8207617
Email: arlenhouse@gmail.com

Distributed internationally by
SYRACUSE UNIVERSITY PRESS
621 Skytop Road, Suite 110
Syracuse, NY 13244–5290
Phone: 315–443–5534/Fax: 315–443–5545
Email: supress@syr.edu

ISBN 978–1–85132–018–9, paperback
(a signed and numbered limited edition is also available)

Typesetting ¦ Arlen House
Printing ¦ Brunswick Press
Cover Images ¦ Peta High, astrologer
Máighréad Medbh

Contents

AUTHOR'S NOTE

Many people are sceptical of astrology, understandably, especially considering the whimsical confetti that passes for it in the popular press. I studied it for three years and it captured my interest and respect. The natal chart can be astoundingly accurate in identifying personal characteristics and the general progress of a life, though how it does this I can't fathom. The 'weather' in a life can definitely be predicted, if not exact events.

I'm not a professional practitioner, and this suite of poems is not an argument. However, I'm inclined to point out that astrology has been around, in one form or another, for about five thousand years, and I'm by no means the first poet with an interest in it. Louis MacNeice went so far as to write a book about the subject, and W. B. Yeats was chairman of the incipient Irish Astrological Association in the 1920s.

The concept behind the collection was to map my dreams in relation to the moon's monthly passage through the twelve zodiacal signs. The moon remains in each of the signs for just over two days at a time. I wondered if I would, say, dream of conflict when the moon was in Aries, or of children when it was in Cancer. I recorded my Morphean meanderings and they did sometimes bear up the appropriate astrological themes. It could only have been scientific over time, but at any rate I had enough interesting oneiric experiences to begin a collection of poems.

Twenty of these poems describe dreams. The others are poems of the night and half-light, and they are not all auto-biographical. They have been allocated what seemed the appropriate signs.

In the end, the zodiac provided the structure for a narrative that explores some aspects of the generation as well as my inner life. In my lifetime there has been a shift from the sacrosanct notion of a solid home to an acceptance of relationship insecurity. We have lifelong learning and mobility where we once had jobs-for-life. Slower avenues of communication have morphed into the worldwide information superhighway. We have been shunted from womb to weather, from home to homies, from bed to bedlam. Hence the sequential arrangement: I start with Cancer, sign of the mother, ruled by the moon, and finish with Gemini, the sign of communication, ruled by Mercury. There is a domestic feel, but then, most dreams happen at home.

Twelve Beds for the Dreamer

CANCER

Moonface

You would expect heat,
but her face is luminous, not blazing.
She had scuttled behind the curtain
until the shaft came
that paralyses and displays.
Smile, you're on TV.
Smile, you're pinned in a glass case.
Shine, you're a trophy.

She prefers to sit in the dark,
where she has no face.
It goes without saying
that dark is the prime source
and that it contains answers,
if only it could know itself.
She lies back and lets time flow through her,
turns the breath of her inners to tides,
contemplates her lone importance
and the subtle spread of her feet.

She's a watcher in the dark,
a waiter you can't summon.
No click or yell or thump
will displace her.
And when you don't see her,
how can you tell if she
is mustering her troops?

FALLING

Where the land ends in a blind drop
he's gone skittish
patter skip hop scuttle
everything's a breeze
nothing to a dive
might as well be a soft bed
where he somersaults.

He's a rushing creature
swift as any pack-backed beetle
less sense less sense.
Don't you know when there's an end to the track?
Don't you know where to stop?

He doesn't stop.
He's done it this time. Gone too far.
I lie and peer over. Cliffs of Moher.
There he is clutching to a scrawny twig
my round son my small chick
my big-eyed seal pup.

I reach and it's not *Space Jam.*
My arm has only one length no extensions.
I'm not *stretchy man.*
Can it be him I see falling
abseiling without the rope?
Maybe he's made of rubber
often seems he is
and his head of steel.
He has banged it off walls and giggled.

It would be better wouldn't it
to reach for independence
harbour power and panache

not be such a mother
such a like-my-own mother?
I was reared to be a carer.
I clustered my daydreams around that.
Now home is the brooch she never wore
the engagement ring that hardly knew her finger
the dishcloth drying over the fire that never blazed
and her hooked upon the hearth
abc-ing her legs trying to suck some solace in.

I like to think I'd fight for my sons
but how far would I risk my neck?
There was a gypsy woman
who crept through the Nazi compound every night
to view her daughter through a chink in the
galvanised iron.
She was only two she said.

Any child could be taken.
I've lain in shiver considering that.
Such happenings are only a trick of space.
I might one day
in the time it takes to get my bearings
see my son go bunji-jumping cordless
and be left without a view
desertly lost
sandily dispersed
with an itch in a raw spot
and a hearth that never fully heats.

Pillow

happy mammy is my pillow
my cushioned slide
my ocean of plastic balls
my raspberry ice-cream
my candy floss cupped in dimples
my fave teddy
my cool runners
my baseball cap turned backwards
my rapid new bat

mammy sad mammy pale
no sleep mammy
mammy looking over my head
like there's a lizard on the wall
mammy holding her cigarette
too near her hair
mammy yelling
mammy burning the chips
mammy crying
whacking the wall
slamming the bedroom door

i won't go to sleep
i have bad dreams
dinosaurs are after my toes
frankenstein has a tent
between the headboard and the wall
and there's a blacker kind of dark draws him out
don't close the door
mammy sitting on the sofa
doesn't move when I stand beside it
even though my eyes are wet

water bursting in
waves lashing at my face
hole in the galley
monster mouth
thought it was a cave
its stomach is big as a bus
tall as a skyscraper
hot as a volcano
and it burns

FULL

apple soft from stewing
cream that stands
sunshiny custard
trifle mattress-thick
chocolate mousse
doughnut at the back of the mouth
sugar in its melting stages
break-down then slide
stomach-bag full and stretching
simply sofa
fit to burst
take more
fill the soup-cup with coffee
slurp milk
a yoghurt couldn't do much harm
you'll make another person here
it's sour to be alone
without a little dish waiting
everyone's leftovers ask to be used
and when you're chock
you're nearer my sin to thee
the aftermush of flavours
rampant on your tongue
you're stretched out on the floor
just one more and you'll really batter the scales

it feels to be full

Home-makers

Homes are made by dreamers,
through whom gestures, expressions,
a shock in the eye,
become stone of the philosopher,
mirrors of an essence,
struck by the sun and ignited
in the dabble of paint brushes.
Splash of colour on paper yearns to butterfly
red, yellow, blue, running purple.
Tomato sauce oozes on cheeks, egg on nose,
teeth gleam white because brushed,
hair is shinily shampooed,
cheek stroked, new sock eased over heel-cut,
hotted bodies are savloned and sponged.
She lies while cublike children examine and crawl;
notes their fiddle at the ear,
pulls precepts from their simply wise,
learns from the stand-up of hairs,
builds sense from sensation,
history from silent time.
Conjures the ben-stone and sits pithy
on the stalk that can't break now.
By matters that reflect the eternal
made adamant.

Homes are made by warriors,
who hack at broken hearthstones,
install new façades,
make compost of organic refuse,
mow the meadow-shy back lawn,
startle the front with paving stones,
fountains, ponds, courts of red roses.
Will talk when parents meet,
make sure neat clothes still fit,

pay to keep body and mind toned,
house buffed to a standard glow.
Here's your face,
renewed by flare of fire,
cleansed by sword swipe, lunge, hoist;
clear-eyed because ground is clear
of stumble-items, things without place.
Build a tower here and the marrow packed within,
grown and nurtured inch by dense inch.
She makes move, nothing left to settle;
no mould grows because moulds can make old.
Take dust and throw it to the past.
The pillar of light moves on.
By straitened ways and passion made perfect
become the spine.

LEO

Sister Sun

The frizzle-haired sun will draw your eyes
and then say no to looking except askant;
makes mirrors of glossed presses, buffs kitchen tiles,
changes the colour of draining cups
long before you struggle to the routine;
spreads marmalade over the perisphere
and peach juice;
why you reach for orange and lemon
to spirit you first thing,
push rays down throat gone jagged from beer
and too much inhalation.
You have no little light without the mage.
Lower your prospect beneath her giving –
so pure, so perfect, so utterly living –
you dare not reach into her face.

Secret Rites

(The word 'orgy' is derived from Greek, via Latin 'orgia', meaning 'secret rites' or 'revels')

The division between us, the crack in my armour,
is what you bend to adore.
You slide your finger in, push your plunger in.
In the pushing you're formal, a kind of logistics
employed –
how far, at what angle, how strong the thrust,
how long the circling and preparation.

I can't stand the challenge when it's a game of skill.
I prefer some ineptitudes:
a ham-legged dance; awkwardness of manner.
But you must observe this rite:
first
circle me thrice and be aware that I am special,
that my genetic code is one in 7.87 trillion Caucasians
and that a singular point in time and space is occupied
by me;
second
know that you and I are not grains of sand to be
thrown together,
rolled over, moved on, always part of some new dune,
that we will shape and build the other, adding or
detracting with each touch;
third
draw closer and decide that if this is only a night,
we'll make it a chandelier full of crystalled eyes.

WARNING! XXX HARDCORE MATERIAL
Hi guys, I'm Peaches. I am a country girl from Montana
but my intent is to be a show girl. I have only been in Las
Vegas for a few months and took a job as a stripper to keep
up on my moves. I'd love to show you what I can do.

You can fly to an island off Spain
and recreate with all the frenzy of a loaded pocket,
all the glory of a beach umbrella.
That's the land of vine and honeys,
where everyone's booty is on show.
Down on the beach you can pick him up,
lay her down like oranges, peel each other and suck.
New one then; never eat the same orange twice.
You make love to the edging of sunrise
and imagine yourself in *The Sheltering Sky*
or *Nine and a Half Weeks*,
except you only have two.
Cram cram.

Perhaps there was no time
you could hope for simple devotion –
an upfront, never failing *I accept you* –
that love-song propaganda.
But, sceptic though I am, I wait by the side of orgies,
still believing a thought out of that swarm
will render me the one.

Son – A Triptych

Everlasting Boy

i'm an everlasting boy
i jump on toys and they don't break
i'll never have a cut that kills
or an ache that won't evaporate
i don't need what other boys need
no good food just sweets 'n sweets
don't need toilets don't need to wash
i'll never get dirty or old or fat
i'll feed on *bruisers* and *blackjacks*

i'm an everlasting boy
can fight a monster
kick him in the arse
cut his head off
throw him up to mars
i never walk away when I'm afraid

i'll be a gymnast when i'm big
and everyone will say
not that i care
that i'm great
like fionn
come back to break records
come back to fight burglars
come back to be the only everlasting boy

Man Cub

From the mountain and the great grey bulk
moves too in the muscles at his shoulders.
He's the sleeping mighty when his heart is downward.

now a monkey now a cheetah now a kangaroo
he's a pussycat put his milk in a bowl
if it spills he'll have it on the floor
lick it up lap lap it
if you get a laugh by running naked on the green
do it

His toes have eyes made to study close
the hidden creatures at roots.
He trusts every step,
dashes from place to time in a personal adventure.
Timmytan of Tin Tin Street –
his mammy lets him do everything.

We have the measure of him here in the suburbs,
where houses are weeds and nature's in miniature.
We shove on shoes as grids for his feet,
give him toy fields to run in, toy animals to feed.
No infusions of the vast, no great heights, canyons,
tornadoes, volcanic ash, sun rising over plains
to feed him back his knowledge.

Well, take up your pen, splatter your paints,
make something special of your *marla,*
see elephants in bicycle handlebars
and spacemen in the fall of your *k'nex.*
Run naked through the house and know that –
yes you said it – the sun is God.

EARTHLING

Christ, but you walk steady on the earth,
shoulders square to it, feet sure as if wild.
Your flesh calls to the planet's
like a peeled apple, a ripe pear,
a lone bear on the mountain.

Eyes screwed up, face gone,
in tears you come crashing hundreds of feet
to a bellowing river where you are lost.
Knife-bearing enemies around you and there's
no protector.
One boy the last hope of the world.
Your body is battle-up, knees bent,
pulling away from me in this midnight terror.

Mostly you're lion cub, bounding down the hall,
jumping up to lick your father's face,
curling to my lap as if it were yours,
examining what shines, planning the next amazement,
every laugh so fully here it trips the house.

You wear rapid tracksuits, *Action Man* shirts,
baseball caps turned backwards.
You're a cool dude, a Kung Fu fighter.
You can bang your head against a wall
and not be hurt. You won't be run over,
you're stronger than car or truck.

You say you were Chinese last time.
This time you believe in tigers
and anything that's furious.
Your element is fire.

LION'S PLAY

What would I do rising from a sun-dream but make love to you as a lion? You bite into my hair not knowing where it orangeful came from when it had been clipped. It's all over the place now and you can't get away from it. It's giving you electric shocks. You keep twitching and throwing small convulsions like you can't stay and you can't not.

I like my lionface. It's wide and still pointed. The nose is the best part. It sniffs not petty sniffs like a human nose but sniffs that trawl long distance. I whiff the sprung spring of a man two miles away.

Come back to you and your round bouncy skin bags full of juice loosey feeling ready to spill yeah yawn. Lions always yawn I always yawn when I want you. Under the awyawning my legs are in a Y and all my lips are opening wide. Come into my jaws my maw. There's a nice prey. I'll throw myself over you coatlike and with great furry hands on your shoulders hold you down. You're mine. I have you now. You're not going anywhere. I'm coming onto you raking you in perhaps bleeding you but you like it don't you. Plaything happy balls bounce bump smooth leap reach for the main thing the upper echelons top of the food chain. Nothing eating me now.

VIRGO

Plants

1. Catherine

My mother is always moving.
Even sitting is a form of work
where she listens and cultivates,
much as she might prune a laurel
or set another bright flower for the summer.
The rockery in the corner of the yard
is a wilderness made formal
for love of the human race.

Scene One
She's hanging net curtains,
sliding them onto their springy spines,
fold pushing fold like a worm fleeing a bird.
When they're up two holes gape and the netting sags.

In he comes at her back
– like when he threw the milk
or crept up and slapped her behind –
and makes to hit her for her sin,
tearing the curtains, wasting money as usual.
He sees me.
Something about me, she used to say,
could calm him down.
Instead of hitting, he slaps two silver disks
on her back and marches out happy.
He can always track her now.

Scene Two
He's standing in my present bedroom.
So is she, as if it were theirs.
He's humbler, eyes down,
saying sorry for all the times.

Unlike before, she won't forgive.
She holds her shoulders like epaulettes
and points him to his wrongs,
how he has stolen her life.

Scene Three
I'm dancing in a home-made video,
singing *Bye Bye Miss American Pie,*
and my face is apple-round.
In a sudden switch,
I have survived cancer and hair-loss
to climb a mammoth wooden staircase,
knowing that somewhere above
my two daughters sleep
in their outdoor clothes.
Their minder is careless,
does only what she must.

Unlike Catherine, my mother,
who now lies dying down the hall,
past the bathroom with a sunken bath
and deep steps toeing the water.
She would have washed them as she did us,
in a small plastic tub
she'd fill from saucepans and kettles,
or standing in their underwear before the fire,
their feet in balmy basins.
She would have aired pink lawn-cotton nightdresses
on the *Waterford* anthracite contraption
and eased them on over their unruly, fly-away hair,
which she would then have brushed a hundred times,
scouting for nits.
She might have made soup,
the long fingers of steam tickling their noses,
masking their cheeks with red petals.
If it were cold, she would have had them wear socks,

or put a hot water bottle between the sheets
just beyond their toes.

In the sickbed her face is white and her hair
gossamers around it,
as if she will now become someone else.

2. Uriel

So it was you took my mother's ring,
pretending to be friendly, but cuckoo,
saying you were a neighbour.
You and your wife stayed too long,
moved the hands of my clock by telekinesis,
made things disappear – me too.
I was locked outside my own house
without her engagement ring that I always wore.
You even charmed the policeman.
But I discovered your weakness.
Water thrown in a heavy stream
reduced you to eyes and mouth.
In the last inkling of your existence
I asked your name.
Uriel, you said.

Note

The above dream came in two parts as I've described, but at the time I had no idea that Uriel is connected in astrological lore with Mercury, messenger of the gods. Nor did I know that his element is said to be fire and that he has been represented as the angel who stood at the gates of Eden to expel Adam and Eve.

Medicine
(for Anthony)

To dream of a tiger or a standing bear is big medicine.
We've had ours in the field-mice and bees,
and the lighting glimpse of a hare
in the covert of the legendary fox.

We've played in our dreams' demesne,
stood by the fairy fort invisibly joining hands.
I've watched you when you didn't know,
to send mothering out like she would.
You've calmed my nerves
with kinder truths and disprin.
Yes, you've helped my pain.

And if the glaring yellow lines of man-done time
should come breaking things in parts,
we can swallow this capsule and sink safe –
into the christmas mornings
and the nights of booze
and the songs we sang anyway
and saturday afternoons in o'neills'
and the certainty that the place still holds
where we were home.

Last

It won't last, because nothing
How do you know how long exactly this is taking?
Is it
mean
sidereal
tropical
standard
summer
solar
lunar
gross menstrual time?

How many days was it on Jupiter,
whose great red spot – your red hot love –
has stormed for three hundred our years at least?

Two hundred and sixty-four thousand
four hundred and sixty Jupiterian days
of nine hours and fifty-five minutes
the spot has been visible.
That's one hundred and nine thousand
five hundred and seventy-five earth days
of twenty-three hours fifty-six minutes
four point zero seconds mean solar time,
but I rounded a figure off, so that's not exact.

Venus takes two hundred and forty three earth days
to rotate on its axis. *Oh what a night.*
The universe is thirteen billion years in the making;
think of all that attrition and contrition.
Because planets rotate,
is that why we make this question our poor doll pivot
and that tune our only comfort:
ah, but will it last?

LIBRA

Deep Night

In the spacey nutshell of deep night
you come to bed with a hot-water-bottle,
because I'm always asleep
and working this late on the Internet
leaves something in you cold.

I'm messed up in dreams,
held by no grudge now.
My name has changed
and my earth-looking parts are craving
like any animal's, wanting to be fed.

I wrap you like a blanket,
hold you in a prison of flesh,
feel your face and hair with enormous fingertips.
Drawing your shoulders huge as the moon,
I let my roots and yours speak their own moves,
ask your branches to visit
in the generous trunk that houses lives.

In deep night everything mates,
no questions asked,
until the morning's talk
comes sundering again.

CHINA

Earth echoes in a Chinese museum,
where great crucibles and sculpted ids
make blue and white a telling fashion,
light and fissile as joy.
Everything teeters,
but in a break would scatter easy pieces,
small scuds on the mirroring floor,
of laughs, bubbles, giggles and shrugs.

This dream is a bead for my memory chain
I will rub and wrap my tongue around,
letting taste and fizz transmit
to flagging nerves and sad somatic cells,
so I can believe something will change.
More chain than jewel these past five years.
I've been shouting, seeing through promises,
hacking the normal, cutting off ties,
turning beauty to ideologue,
discharging honesty gut to gut,
baring my teeth,
snarling at the half-door.

From the museum to a hotel
I drift like a wisp with three good friends.
We lounge and the walls humour us,
leaning to hear our talk.
He's sweet, the dark one, head lowered
in shy wit and respect.
These two deep beds could meet in a flash
and we'd not mind the crowding.
So when the girl calls it's a normal thing,
a job she does like waitressing or managing a shop.
She's young, hair black as clubs, eyes kohled,
shimmied into red silk.

We talk like friends. She's a student,
pays her fees by making east meet west,
conjuring the globe for leisured liberals like us,
who nod.
My woman friend and I will leave.
The girl can have two, what odds?
As I pass, she turns as if to ask
how we can walk and browse while she works.
I stop, and when I do
it's I who shimmy in red silk,

turn slim, then schoolgirl, then black pleats
then smooth black hair and a job I do with my body,
while my heart spins and casts its arteries –
down the street to the china archives,
red streams under tourists' feet,
red streaks among the white and blue.
Ebbing back in a flair of colour
to deliver what's needed, what's due,
what anyone deserves –
a piece of clay formed into a planet,
held like a safe place, near enough to be home.

Atomic Goddess

o don't
comb your careless red hair
with splayed fingers
tips touching your scalp
don't
like the *clairol* ad
the *wash 'n go* ad
the way you're sweeping it up
and heaping it on your head
ignoring
don't ignore
the strand beside your ear
that will flutter like a flag
to proclaim you only care so much
or that your symmetry is so fine
we need a swinging rope to climb up

your arms are pure gold
i'd like to roll them in my palms
and press my cheek to them as if
standing unsecuritied in a fine art museum

don't
fold that river up
leaving the nape of your neck
like a silky toy waiting to be touched
talisman of flesh
how could anyone resist
the prospect
the
sheer-cliffs-don't-care-i'm-jumping-fuck-the-parachute
promise in you
each atomic goddess pressing to be unbound
from the breathing bun and bundle of your crown

Crush

When Guy wants sex, he slinks
in silence to where she fits bracelets and rings.
She brushes her eyebrows, spikes her hair,
searches through drawers for tights to go
with the dress.
He lies on the bed and pinches her shirt,
rubbing bobbles the washing made.
He stretches his finger to pencil her back,
in search of a language, a telepathic picture
of the world she has come from.
Remembering then the feel
of a jacket he would have preferred,
but a rich cousin owned it.
Jiggles her breasts, head down,
a grin on sideways.
This is like the day of the altar wine.
He drank it quickly while the priest de-robed,
his face so sweet you'd never have guessed.
He slinked away then like he winds around her,
a banished pariah, head flat as tail,
no end or beginning, a begging thing,
whose only power is to crush or be

SCORPIO

Under

I might have been white as lightning,
no dark spikes shadowing my ears.
I might have been innocent,
not harbouring the harsh word
nor the cold that spreads its tendrils,
miniaturing the house.

But I came with dark foundation,
top half struggling to be lotus,
nether half in swamp.
That's why I twitch when my feet touch a glass floor
and there's no scandal beneath,
why I crook over on the river bank,
dive through the covering moss
scatter the settled water lilies,
descend until I've known what it's like to drown.

Suckers lift the skylight.
I peer down to where a baby outlined in thick black
floats stiff and half-sunken in a limpid bath.
Great white tiles are rimmed with black,
the baby's skin white.
Something takes my shoulder
and I'm plucked into a cave-like face
that calls seekers to its hollows.

No fear keeps me stiff or silent in the bed.
When in a second I decide, I proclaim my stand,
banish to its cronies the unbrookable thought
that thinks I'm shiny, full of spirit nosh,
worth binding in its web and sucking.

It withdraws as quickly as it came,
but there are others waiting,
a team to push me under,
take me close to strangled babies
and the pain I might love.
They won't tell me to dam my eyes.
They'll give me night vision
and send me plunging.
Until I can find some channel
and a clarifying guide to swimming high,
breaking through where you'd think was stagnant,
breathing light.

ECLIPSE

Sunhair suncheek sunlip sunglazed limbs.
Seen her on streets
hipsway tease.
Followed her track my eyes did
jumped out and bounced after
bounced until she turned the corner
lenses on her all the time
taking in
her sunlilt sunroll to the right and left.
She doesn't ask for attention she gets it
holds it like her jeans hold her
like her jumper hugs her.
Bodies like hers don't need designer clothes.
Plain blue doesn't phase a star.

She's been shot.
She's a wrap.
Candid video ripe for re-showing.
Edited dickied up.
Playing on the retina big time.

roll it

She's here
no longer walking.
Ours now
a gang of indiscriminate sex.
We throw her down
I willing too
shave her sunhair bare to the baseglow
mount her from behind and use her like a doll.
Something in her capture is a thriller.
I don't think beyond the simple plot.

the film stops

I have to tell a friend.
He mutters kindly
'The subconscious does strange things'.
I try to believe there's no part of me
would shave a sun of every ray
disregard a totem
turn movement to a slice of flesh
ride rough-shod
ever slash a smile
into a soiled and broken body
like a god.

Nick Cave Makes Love To Me
(Dreamscene)

Little mother when I make love to you
I'll scatter petals to your breasts –
domestic flowers that you never set –
sweet peas, peonies, laurels, violets.
I'll hold your knickered bottom in my hand
and kiss it like an apple with the stalk still.

I'll lick and stroke and maybe rub my teeth
along the veined marshmallow plains
of your thighs untoned and ghostly white.
Lifting thumb against your clit,
I'll raise you up like rivers on my head,
de-icing and creating in a generous swarm.

Little mother when I make love to you
I'll hold your knickers in my hand
and smell the juices you can't help but cook,
a mix of carelessness and school.
Your secrets are deep red and full,
like the inner parts of rhubarb tarts and purple plums.

'I can stay up for a fair good time',
I tell you as I probe the wet.
You bring my sex into your open home,
as a pillar to its bone foundation.
Bite me like the wolf you often are,
away from pack and practised in the loneliest desire.

Little mother I can bear your scars.
I can carry them away.
When we come to drown ourselves in slush
I'll remember what you said:
'Did you have enough to eat?' 'Are you cold?'

Little mother things that make us all afraid
and want to sex it out to Hell.
Little motherbrother of my songs,
come with me.

Night On Valencia Island

Dark feeds on the livers of children,
sours the food in stomachs,
bores holes behind the lobes,
winds craftily into spaces
that were safe inside the eyes.
If I don't move I could end up in a wriggle,
struggling futile against the pin.

I fear the Skellig and the trip,
the great convulsing jelly of sea
wanting bodies to sponge it before it sets.
The thought keeps me awake,
as others have in their night,
trepidations before tiny steps,
no-faith face to the universe.

What if in this blind space, now,
a violence were done?
My child turns in bed, then walks the dark.
I reach for the lamp switch, hope I don't meet a hand.
I part the curtains for some shine from the harbour.
There's a false tone to everything I do,
habitually pretending I can.

Milk and *Thick Tea* biscuits buoy me this time.
Then back to blankets with the kitchen light still on.
As if that imitation of day were enough
to blast the mines
and light me to treasure or the grave.

An Ordinary Lane

Ten minutes ago this was an ordinary lane,
if any place with green lightning strokes
piled upon each other as if they were hair
made jungle by no combing
could be called ordinary.

Ten minutes ago this was anybody's track.
You could stand at the entry,
knowing down the street by your left ear
was an everyday line of houses,
and your right eye could back a little
to snap Murphy's local shop
with its *bluckjacks, bruisers, penny jellies,*
pushpops, taytos and *hula hoops,*
that was so tempting, just knowing it was there.

This lane could be the journey of your liking.
You could pretend –
adult or child could pretend –
you were where?
France, Africa, China, the rebel countries,
highways with no natural foundation.

Ten minutes ago, turning into this lane
meant starting to bud,
spouting in the non-vernacular.
Why are you not a tree?
You could have leaves like tens-of-spades
expressing you.

You could pick blackberries,
clusters but all one,
eat them like memories,

their boundaries and unity
pasted on the heave of your tongue.

Ten minutes ago.

Now there's red, splurging where it's tender,
black lines hacking through a rapid flux.
This is not the toothache from too many sweets.
So new this sore you can only scream,
but you're choked.
Either move or breathe.
Someone must come.
This creature makes your heart convulse.
All the fight you have, like the seed
that with the utmost drive insists on constant charge,
made you grow supple, founded in unshakeable soil,
but now can't give you choice
to keep this lane an act of collection
where you gather to yourself your tender millennia.

Ten minutes ago this lane was yours.
Now here's your deepest drain.
Stunned by the face of silence,
it muzzled its scream.

SAGITTARIUS

Big Bong

in thunder comes the breath of outer space
a ringing bell but bellring never reached
the deadline for departure is no time
nowhere precisely on no day a stray
event a chance to be a finite some
the noise makes nothing clear says nothing safe
and every hold is blown with eructation

the somehow always sucking in has stopped
full lung is pain and pain is endless sound
it gets so thick and hot no tube can last
we make the spew of no direction home
get slow we're here and home's a caravan
collision quake we knock spots off our face
that ride with us and make our spin a path

we look at where and how far we're away
we make relations see how big we bear
a round a wheeling make a pattern sing
the same old thing we like the same old thing
we always sang but never thought the tune
was measured and repeated fugue on fugue
our knowing is a no to knowing no

division between being and the void
we'd unite again all of us would mush
if daisies didn't push the soil apart
volcanoes didn't burst and storms distend
slim rains go shadow-battling grass go gold
sly flora grow on half an inch of crust
new babies berries honey and the hive

a thunder takes the insides and the eyes
become a way to eat a hut to hide

the smallest thing looks outside for itself
reflections of its manner and its mind
when enemies have died come eat their flesh
one bite and innocence dissolves to run
again as hunger and the jabbing spear

to represent the provenance of touch
the lurch the burst unbearable enjoy
slipsoar and maybe never feel again
make ecstasy a prime noetic thing
too large to hold too large to let it go
in spread a mappa mundi fold a ball
we venture into darkness and we draw

conclusions build a hall with massive rise
project our image make the image good
we've learned division we create again
a mirror of our feardom and our dream
live in beneath enormous roofs that splay
and vaunt and play the part of some sad reach
that thinks it touches glory with a bell

Sad-Eyed Sunday

Sad-eyed Sunday slinks again,
comes spancilling my legs.
I stumble. No place to fall.
I can't get past breakfast,
hang over my guidelines.
Such an aching day –
the marathon stretch in her,
yellow, pale blue about the edges.
She has nothing to do,
purrs like teenagers in the sun,
hangs out with them at the local shop,
smokes a long brown thin cigarette,
looks me in the face and says,
'If you're not happy you're a moron.
What kind of fool would let a day meant for stretch
go tight and shrink to a thin rag about her ankles?
What an ass.
What a silly abandoned ill-fitting humourless clueless
inept conglomeration of maladjusted components you
are'.
Sunday's a bitch.

Bound

You could say I clung to a fat fish,
swimming at quiet depths,
where things by some perversion of the eye
were seen in only black and white,
although the sea was teeming with colour,
endlessly diverse.

I had to wrench myself from the simplicities:
good/evil;
love/hate;
truth/falsehood;
life/death;
for me/against me.

Can I float, alone and only bedded by the air,
among the unkept chronicles of space,
questions at every turn?
Must stay cagey.
What I live for escapes me.
The body holds when the mind thinks go.

In my dream I'm dragged struggling to the people.
I'm thrown among them,
accounting for myself as the gallows is hammered.
I wake to silence, endemic hypocrisy,
and a huge wheel I'd like some room upon.

Mages of Surge

Mages of surge work in numbers and alone.
No speech is required.
They share the same mind,
move to a huge beat.
They arrive when you call.
You have chosen and your choice
needed no deliberation then,
which is now,
which is forever.

Mages of surge emanate
from blue and grey undersea halls,
from mundane bedrooms,
council flats and Hollywood mansions.
For each cell of thought or fact
they provide the same urge,
concentrated or diffused,
the key to quintessence,
knowing without analysis,
analysis with some basis.

They will give you one picture, give a maze,
lead you, understand you, let you drive.
They don't need you to adore.

Storm

1 *From a Bedroom window*

Why do I feel I'm looking at a picture
when the thing itself is on display?
Outside the window, an ash with the figure of a model
has been injured by the casual swipe of a freak storm.
One branch hangs asking,
weeps into the lap of a glowing begonia hearth.
The plant tolerates well the uninvited bellows
reaching into its enclave to fan its tips.
This is the closest I get to wild.

2 *National Geographic*

A tiger stalked the sambars
until her sides were sunken
from shoulder blade to haunch.
Finally, the wind allowed her close enough
for her favourite event, the sprint.

She needed that kill so much
not even small birds were allowed to take a morsel.
She slept beside it.
In the night a greedy male
dragged the body to his own patch,
its weight etching blood into the tracks.

Waking to an empty lair, she hardly blinked,
but directed her face, inscrutable as grass,
to where the male, on higher ground,
lifted his upper lip and snarled.

She stretched her limbs as though she were alone
and had no appointments with food or enemy.
Shaking the dust from her paws, she strolled away
and found a waterhole to bathe her underparts.
When washed, she stalked again and ate,
no sun sinking on her loss.

A sister had fought for her kill
and ended with a window to her flesh,
a flap of skin like a flag of surrender
hanging with her as she went.

By such diversity movements are made.

CAPRICORN

Scene 1: The dressing-room of a large theatre. Athene, an academic, part-time performer of political songs and poetry, and Medusa, an old woman.

Athene:
You were late for the sound-check, you smelly old bitch. What was I like, alone and fussing, my hands on a go-slow, couldn't get the foundation on right, without a brush to give my cheeks that earthy glow. I'm not earthy by nature. I like to assess how things work, how things should work. Logistics are my specialty. Everything runs better as a military operation. That's what you don't realize. Five means five and seven means seven. What were you doing, sunning your serpents?

Medusa:
It may come as a surprise to you, but old women have pleasures too. One of them is keeping people waiting.

Athene:
I'd behead you again if I could, you useless hag. You're like a worm, growing your face back like that, reclaiming it as if it were still your logo. It's not. Perseus and I won it. You had no right to take it from my t-shirts without a clean fight, but then you always fought dirty.

Medusa:
You might have known, you of the acrobatic intellect, that everything reverts to its rightful owner, one way or another. History is a Ferris wheel and you can't always be at the top. Sometimes you have no view and

all you can do is stare into the glazed face of the ticket seller while your seat swings and goes nowhere.

Athene:
If I could do without you I would. Look, I'll pay you. I have quite a good income. Let me buy the franchise on your face. I've asked you before. You know it's not impossible. And I'm sure you could do with the money to feed your profligate habits.

Medusa:
As usual, your ego misleads you. I have no need of your money. I always have enough because I take what I want, quietly, not like you, stalking in with the shotgun on your arm. I sit on the island with my sisters and women come to us, women who are grateful for our healing and protection. We know who we are. You haven't got a clue. You've done wonders for this man-made society of yours, poured into it your scientific expertise, your skill in technology, and made it prosperous. But you won't bring children into it, will you? You work with men but you won't mate with them. I wouldn't mind but you won't mate with women either. Your heart is a clock. Arrive at five, arrive at seven, arrive at nine! But when you want art you turn to me, you always turn to me. You know what I do, but you neither emulate nor appreciate. Times have changed. For years you could wear my face on your breast without looking at it yourself. Pretending you were teaching wisdom but never going past the essential threshold. Go out now and bare your vagina on the stage. Show them the pubic hair that reaches to the knees. Take the cock out of your mouth and speak.

Athene is called to the stage. She and Medusa look at each other in silence for some seconds. This is an old battle. One time Athene would have had more allies, but there has been a groundswell of change and the new ranks hold no proper definition for her. She doesn't know who to fight for any more, so she's trying to fight for herself. It's a lonely task. The women perform the usual ritual. They stand with palms pressed together and a transfusion occurs which is marked by a shudder through each. Medusa's features draw themselves onto Athene's t-shirt.

Athene:
But why do you always come?

Medusa:
Remember your mother, and how your father's roaring always shut her up? So much so that her throat seized and in the end she only whispered, manically focused on table items, whether she still had all her forks and small spoons, how to get the stain out of the table cloth, folding and re-folding the towels in the hot-press. You broke away, sneaked out the back window and ran. You thought of great things then, the fellowship of women, the lifting of stereotypes, an overhaul of the economy. You did great things, you were an inspiration. You're still an inspiration, although you've never properly defined your direction. That day you first saw me, my face floating towards you as you lay tired and worn out, you couldn't take it. I was a beauty in everyone's eyes and all I wanted was fun. Out every night, shifting men, slicing through your ideologies, painting myself, dying my hair. You couldn't look at my face, so you gave yourself a reason to hate me, made me ugly. What you didn't know is that, being immortal, you would live to see that ugliness turn to style. I was

surprised myself when my sisters brought me back to life with my own blood and told me that my face would be prized by the women of this age.

Second call for Athene. Her make-up is in sweat-streaks on her face.

Medusa:
Go on. What you're about to say on that stage is true. My image will provide the rest.

Scene 2: The auditorium, shaped like an amphitheatre, is huge. To the left, the bar is frilled with noisy drinkers. Nearer the stage there are tables covered with red cloths and people from many nations are clapping slowly, waiting for the show. When Athene arrives, she hears her name spoken and echoed. She begins. The words of the songs are raw, like glimpses of her inner organs – a bleed from the liver, a kidney overflow, a burst heart vessel, a bulging womb. All through, a hundred bar-huggers maintain a loud hum of conversation. She never wins them, although she yells enough to make her throat raw. A gathering at the front likes her, especially a French married couple who pound their table. It's not enough. It's as if the grey bowl of the theatre were crushing her; she feels it slowly closing in. She's singing without conviction. The granite-toned Medusan shadow doesn't descend as it should. The audience should be silent as stone, to erupt in colour again once the set has finished. All this time and she's no better than a support act. She bows anyway and maintains her composure. Offstage she presses herself to a wall, her face a rain of make-up, her jeans clinging sweatily, like children. Whatever happens, she can't cry in front of the hag.

Scene 3: The dressing-room again.

Medusa *(taking back her face):*
Don't worry. It's another beginning. Nothing can be by proxy in these times. What you give can't be borrowed or contrived. You'll arrive. Your greatest asset is your dissatisfaction. And I love you, you know.

Athene looks at her sharply. She believes this, at least, to be a lie.

Medusa *(stopping as she exits):*
One day your face will be just like mine. You won't worry then what side you're showing, or whose heart, even if it's your own, is turning to stone.

Daddy Married Me

It must have been an all-male ceremony I wasn't allowed to attend because this is the first I've known of it and it seems a given fact. He's standing there by the inner door getting his coat on with first a jerk and then a sweep about his hulkish chest. I know what's on that chest – spidery orange hairs that curl and twist until they're the jungle that chokes his heart.

Later I'll lie in his bed stiffly on those sticky browning sheets trying to switch off my senses, telling myself I don't feel what will shortly make me vomit – his barrels of fingers, his slabbed hands, the bristle on his chin, the smell of oils and Vaseline, old tar and his spotted pan-shaped thighs. He'll force me because nothing I know finds pleasure in him. He says goodbye to my silent sons. His look says, 'I'm the boss and you'd better not move from here'. He leaves.

I haven't moved, seems I've never grown. There has been no avenue out. All my life I've been governed by him. Married one way or another. There's no doubt but that this house with the close walls is where I'm at his mercy. Me and my children. Whom he owns.

I wake and remember that none of this is true. There's a man beside me. He and my father are not even alike – one small and sandy, the other tall and equine; one dipped in Zambuk, the other steeped in Radox. Still, for a time the dream pervades and there's no difference in the air, no happy story.

Dream of a Yellow Wolf

Her face is close to mine.
I can see how she got here,
how she worked her way through the wood
with unrested sense,
hiding, then finding food.

Though her pack doesn't want her, she'll survive.
She carries their rejection
in the deeper burrows of her fur,
letting it discolour her only a little.

She has walked alone for endless no-change days
and the pain is sometimes less.
You can see the rough sadness in her eyes
and the threat in her naked teeth.
You can't lack this much and not seethe.

She has learned.
Being timid was never the way to gain respect.
When the need takes her
she'll kill without thought,
then rest, fellowless, in the clearing.

Her fur is dirty yellow.
Nothing to be vain about.
She could fade but for two things –
her love of new prey
and her body's manic clinging to itself.

She knows she's a killer.
That leaves her free for kindness
the odd time,
to a human or a bird.
She doesn't fret that she wasn't born generous.

AQUARIUS

ALIENS

We are no more like the polyglot god
than those beings were like you,
and no less.
You made them not in your image
but in your imagination.
Here's how.
You wanted to paint presence without form,
so on a white page you made splashes of colour,
rubbed them out and drew over the traces
a spaceship you had seen on Star Trek.
It was when you stamped on it
that their presence was fulfilled.

They came invisible to inhabit my house.
I knew they were here by the arbitrary movements
of inanimate objects.
There goes the wooden elephant
and that blue Bristol Cream bottle that did for a vase.
I employed two psychics, one melon-haired, one dark.
The first had a line between her eyebrows
and a worried glare in her ionised eyes.
The other wore baubles and a gown too long not to
catch
as she moved between the table and chairs.

Something was worked and I saw the melon-haired
change to a glass globe and float.
I understood then that the strangers
could assume our image.
What they saw they copied.
An old man, one of them, went shimmying out
over the harbour on a thin wire.
When he got to the deepest spot
I stood on a balcony, stretched my hands

and mimed pushing him under.
Down he went.
But before I hauled away, up he rose,
buoyant and laughing on the water.
The balcony dissolved.

It seemed then that dividing lines needed a deep
eraser
and that many more miles had to flit
before we could see between the image and the page.

Angels
(for Máire)

Buried in this mountain of tasks,
deep as the tenton sea that makes fossils from bones,
deep as the ringing core of the earth,
is a place of sweet peace.

Beneath the duties and the physical annoyance,
safe from the necessary weights,
you compose the blueprint of pleasure,
drawing the bright landmarks
of a sheltered expanse.

Birthdays and shiny things possess you,
but angels pull the real strings.
You chatted with them as you walked to school.
One day you'd also fly.
You told me to fear only sin,
that the darkness was a holding hand,
its palm mapping ours.

But how many angels, if they gathered at your door,
would you let in?
How many spirits would you entertain?
How many grains in a pillar of salt?
I think you would have looked back.

Why should you live afraid,
once you've scattered the shadows to a guiding light?
There are dungeons for the grasping angels
those who will not heal,
who raise the hair of others
with their strange-tongued deals.

Millennium

(1990s TV drama series with the slogan:
'This is Who We Are')

Not the human, but the force that drives.
I've met you before, haven't I,
in a different form?
You speak with the same soul.
By Hell you get around.

The wind brooms from pointless angles.
Must we retreat to a previous mind,
disregard so many suns
with their exorcising wands of reason?
This is a compass without a needle —
in our dark room again devising
a monochrome answer to light.

System

Knowledge can be gained in mazed or simple ways:
maybe by the folding of legs,
the circling of thumb and ambition finger;
certainly in pleasure explosions –
one on one makes two times on the table;
yes, knowing you,
knowing a lift-off,
knowing the first rocket.

Dancing to the Dirty Three gives you space in a
ten-by-ten;
energy opens your inners;
let love in and you slice yourself juicily,
sending out the disconnected parts,
so you can be the galaxy
and the spinning planets in their several modes.

Say you have healing then feel it in your fingers;
lay your hands on a back
and remember that matter is crystallised energy.
Put a crystal in the wrong place
and scare the tiny satellites;
turn your inside out,
flip over onto your head
and don't flip back.

The unspeaking child hums,
studies a strand of her hair.
She's captured in her strand of hair
and creates around her such knowledge
that for the first time
we see the system as a strand of hair –
light, ethereal, greatly strained,
what we can't capture – whimsical.

Into the Black

When the time comes to leave a space
I hope I'll not be wanting
and cling like rust to old springs.

This is no time to depend
on horizontal strata, gravity,
or a cushioned cubbyhole in the wall.

Only to stand with angled knees
while the ground sways and uplifts.
Be graceful when your planet forgets its orbit
and goes careering into the great Black.

Be ready to change your colour,
your shoes and maybe feet.
Let go
of backache, varicose veins, depression, headaches,
period pains,
all the ills that keep us full.
Take no prisoners from last year.

X Files
'Trust No One'

There are too many hiding-places.
The back seat of your car is one.
Look in the mirror.
Some stare-faced creature with a sharp knife
might appear like a copycat.
All that will remain of you is a scream.

But when you've gone to where nothing matters,
be comforted that your character
will be re-constructed
and all the good you've never thought of
will be spread on your patch.

Drive on now. And fear.
Because you go to a wobbled home,
where simple comforts like a faithful lover
may be given or taken,
chocolate or poison in a standard issue box.

PISCES

The Emerald Pool

I am no self-contained woman,
no deep-throated, double-breasted
repository of power.
I'm more a puzzled fish, snapping for food
in a sea of uncertain nourishment.
The shark is forever close.
I swim camouflaged,
my mouth pops, my mind spins.

You look from the window.
Outside is a clamorous flux
of words, philosophies, analyses, trends,
well-tended nature, cars, computers,
confident heels, ascending knees, argument,
certain involvement, laughs, love, hope,
other people desiring other people's methods.
But all you are is the spot where you stand,
the spaceship departing in a light-cone,
infusing the message, 'We will return'.
There seems no choice then but to enter
the only portal that remains unshielded.

That's how I came to say yes,
and accept for a time the silence that warps me.
To stand here and watch may be radical too,
as cruel on the gut as fighting;
as hard to be scaled in the still, deep Emerald Pool
as it is to be armoured in the field.

I know that element as if it were skin;
I have floated face up and down,
and once I swallowed some that morphed inside.

I felt it form into a hand-shaped bowl,
that sits here now in a beg,
as if I could bend to a place so internal it's distant.

This is my habit.
I swim, am sleeked, come striding out,
shoulders back, hair pressed to my neck,
my sculpted body a polished teak.
I rest.
Until the trees start a whisper at my back,
the forest begins to cackle
and the sun does nothing to help.
My fingers stiffen, lose their quickness,
mass up like the toes that have begun to arch
and sprout sickles of claws.
My skin turns harsh,
my body convulses and re-forms.

In the Emerald Pool
the image I see shows two new eyes
bulging in my forehead.
My warp-spasm has not phased it.
Sí Gaoithe in the valley
and this cursed pool will only sit prettily green,
waiting to lap me in.
When I open my mouth I don't know if it's to drink
or howl.

The Beauty of the Other Life

A tin of beans and a frozen pizza,
she'll eat those today.
Fast food made to last.

She'll convoy here at the check-out,
behind track-suit bottoms,
in front of blond hair
and kohl-black eye-definer,
impatient to be home.

It's a lovely day, isn't it?
They say it's going to change.
Must go, I want to bring the clothes in.
I have children to collect by three.

The spiritual reader told her
she was once an Egyptian queen
with the rainbow for a hat
and her king was a great warrior
whose spear always struck home,
even when the chariot was at high speed.

She was cruel, she discovered,
watched women raped and children enslaved,
until she grew old and felt her own pain.
She repented then and destroyed herself,
drank a quick, deadly poison,
having divided her jewels among her slaves.

Her health demands she eat salads, fresh wheaten bread.
Instead she'll have a tin of beans and a frozen pizza.
She lives in a white semi-detached,
leafs the pages of *Pi in the Sky*.
The neighbours don't know who she is.

MATTER

I must be touched, no matter by what body,
except there are dog-eyes
and some bridge to nuzzle over.

There's no question but
I'll take your feet on my knees and stroke,
and at three, when all sense has gone to bed,
we'll grope our way to my room,
pausing where you crush me against the wall,
doling all-mouth kisses like thick sponge puddings,
taking me in with vagrant sweeps of your hands.

In the bedroom our clothes take a hike.
I can't see. The condom won't stay stretched.
We fumble like teenagers, can't remember what to do.
Slurps and gasps and hard hugs.
Hurry, so we won't miss the pleasure train.
Blink and it has pulled away,
our fleeting hope of transport
sleepers behind.

There was a man who used to drink his lover's menstrual blood, he said. Revolting, she exclaimed. As soon as he had said it, his eyes grew darker. The whites crushed themselves like gleaming halos against the irises as he stared from beneath the overhang of his eyebrows. His large face turned monstrous in the light sprinkled from the bedside lamp. Everything spread, even the unruly black hair that usually rested in a pleasantly manic mass on his shoulders.

You could be sucked into this one, into his world without *nos*, walls, niches or definitions. She would panic in there, wandering the dark mazes in search of one safe thing. That was why they would split, or was it his squat body, which he said was like a *fear bolg*'s, man of the stomach? Why was it only *Fir Bolg* you heard about? Always plural, like the *Borg*. Maybe they had no individual identities, acted like ants, or water, one drop following the other. The Fir *Borg*. They shook spears and said, 'You will be assimilated'.

He was a good lover, it must be said. And he knew everything, picked up information like a wool jumper does cat hairs. He passed nice comments, such as, 'You don't need eye shadow, your eyelids are lustrous'. On the 'phone time didn't fuss, cushioned itself and purred. So much to say and the past, present and future to say it. For someone needing to talk, she was floored. Well, when you're a swollen heart you don't need one of the same pressed against you like two pigeons making love the wrong way round.

She wished they were pigeons. She had seen them mating on the roof of the railway station. They circled each other, eyes never meeting (he chased her eyes); she did a lot of walking away, looking unconcerned, maybe she wasn't concerned (she'd love to look that unconcerned); he entered her from behind (very sexy when he held her clitoris at the same time; pigeons don't have clitorises). Afterwards they separated and sat some distance apart, still not looking at each other, jerking their heads primly to pretend they were watching many very intriguing moving objects.

She'd like it to be that way, plus clitoris of course, with that cool attitude. Why should a sexual act occupy your mind for ages after, to the point of taking it over? Better to strut away and look off into the distance at something else, because mating wasn't where the satisfaction was. Almost yes, nearly there, oh yes, but it was only a pearl on a necklace that might be more string than jewel. When the ecstasy was over it was back to the plod, which was as great an agony as chaos.

So the best answer was equanimity. Think plod not transportation, string not bead. Must be that she was beginning the pigeon way anyhow, the way she was retreating into the darker corners of her bedsit.

Sac

From walls without colour
feelers tend to follow the outlines of your knees.
They draw the shapes between your toes
and with endings knitted seat your buttocks.
The combing of your hair is a sacred thing.

Where eyes are redundant
and feet have nowhere to go,
silence grows tongues,
the absence of suggestion
honing to hum and itching in the air.
Sometimes there is rhythm approaching slap
without tone at all.
You feel strokes down the lens of your spine
and believe you are content.

Certain issues of light will change you.
They will intrude through the walls
and make you wonder without forming questions.
Now you will hear urgent instructions:
Stay silent. No sudden moves.
Hang on. Don't cut from the root now;
the time is not right, never.

Soon, one of those easing strands that define you
will start to nudge and prod, then another,
until hundreds are at you,
buffeting from all sides, and a tunnel appears.
You will wonder why you never saw it,
then remember how, before the matrix changed,
eyes had been unused.
This is movement
and you'll never know whether it's your wonder
or forces you don't control that caused it.

Well go then,
but this sac loves you,
will always love you,
will wait for you,
sucking all the time.
Allow within its reach
a strand of hair,
a nail-clipping,
the hem of your garment,
and you will belong again.

The only way out is a long dive.
Make it or melt under the sun.

ARIES

A Battle For Peace

I try to leave the house by the front door,
but the woman is there to stop me.
She has short black hair and a bright red top.
She has summoned, before, ten others,
who came when my children were alone.
She directed at a plush distance
as, faceless, they milled through the hall
into the front room.
When I returned I couldn't tell what
damage had been done.

Now she breaks in, despite my say no,
and stands at the bedroom door with forehead aimed.
Next thing I've killed her and I'm fleeing the scene.
All's well until in the lift
I have to fight all over again –
her rabid daughter,
writhing and unselfconscious, tangled hair,
a naked bedlam of flesh and muscle.

I'd like to leave this house by the front door
and know that it will stand,
that I can stroll back in –
having moved to the monkey song
sidestepped on pub seats
hornpiped on tables
somersaulted off and bowed
– and find my children still sitting on a cosy sofa,
the moon in their faces, worry beads flung on the fire,
the warm spoon of home stirring a good one for me.

Lesson

She offers his socks but his hand is away.
He needs it for a fantasy escapade
where he reaches slowly
into an alien tree-bark,
alarmed to every touch,
to find something within that glistens.

A few seconds wait and she snaps.
An offer has been made and derided.
How dare he ignore her, be her daily drag,
flatten her breasts, trail out of her,
swing monkey from her leg?
'WILL YOU TAKE THEM'!

It happens a million times,
each one a screw she tries desperately to un-.
Sometimes the right driver, sometimes not.
It happens without avenue or drive-in.
He says in a small voice she can't hear
because her head's a zoo –
says something she can't hear –
'SPEAK UP I CAN'T HEAR YOU'!

Months later she'll tell him,
'STOP SHOUTING'.
She buckles, because the reason is
she shies away,
rears up,
at the thought of claiming something good.

She knows these alleyways of hers contract and spew,
spatter all round them and scatter friends.
But whether or not she likes what sticks,
she teaches him her lesson.

No Easy Way for Me Yet, Thanks

A pin-striped suit flies away.
I sit with frog-green trees,
grass to lie on, sun to shine in.
There are contacts to be made
in the scrubbed buildings
by the elegant park.
Tanned people think in tow
in interesting cafés,
friends with let-it-out shoulders.

That's nice.
Goodbye.
I'm slipping away by the nearest gap
to the Medusa Breastplate,
more congruous establishment,
where I drink alone.

Lamb

In a large building a woman with military hips
has gathered the orphans,
who shiver in brownish or stained white shifts.
She paces and glares, stops at a four year-old.
'Who was the watcher?' she asks.
'Don't tell', comes the whisper.
The little one cries.
Through splutters and sniffs she gives the name.
The cross is set up, the world goes whirligig,
the girls are sent wheeling,
the informer's eyes are put out.

I fly to mind her,
come down with a blanket of silver,
stay silent with her,
let my heart beat close.
There's life somewhere
if she can weather this.
It's not for me to tell her, is it,
nor for her to hear,
that in some uneasy way
she will always be a lamb.

TAURUS

Stay

Great day it was.
Talk with family you hadn't seen for years.
Picking up where you'd left off.
Learning what everyone's doing now.
Funny stories from the coal-face
of white-collar working.
Until, going home, he loses patience with the child;
the shiny atmosphere corrupts and attacks,
batters the membranes,
strikes the gut with poisoned bolts.

Sit silent in the passenger seat.
You're so goddamned civilised.
You won't fight in front of *her.*
Coward, you don't slam the car door and walk home.
Two weeks later you'd arrive,
having loop-the-looped in transient beds,
wandered through bars, clubs, parties,
and you'd know who you were.

No. You stay, stare away and sulk.
Don't talk. That'll punish him alright.
He doesn't need to talk.
Great torturer you'd make.
But in bed, lie stiff.
Turn your back.
Keep turning your back.
What a waste.

Those curdling clouds, those bolts –
they've possessed you.
Pandemonium.
Scud missiles motoring.
Left brain atrophy.

His mannerisms expand.
Irritating fingers long as Wednesday.
They press the huge red alarm and don't let go.
You're not going to fight, but you're leaving.
You don't love him anymore.
What scheme this time?
What can you see?
The huge sea of possibility.
Possibly you'll be just as alone.
Possibly you'll always be alone.
Maybe the sea won't like you either.
Will spit you back if you try to walk into its mouth.
If you have the guts.
Stay.

It hardly seems like the brink of a new age.

Cowboy

We sat at the same table,
you with your startled eyes,
I head-bowed, shifty.
Never could decide if we were friends or what.
The dining-room was crowded
and when the tremor came,
panic spread like fire on acrylic.
You wanted something done.
You always want something done.

As the earth began to split
I found myself beside my second love,
the one I nearly married, who sat and smiled,
although all society was vanishing
through a fault beside us, including you.

He used to do a cowboy act,
kick open the bedroom door,
come in blazing invisible six guns,
gather me like a sheaf of wheat.

'Well, Cowboy, I live in the big house. My daddy owns this ranch but my car has broken down, so I'll let you give me a lift'.
I invite him in, it's only polite. Up the great, curled, granite steps that flank the door like a handlebar moustache. He's an obvious illiterate, nothing to recommend him but his looks, which mark him as a man of the earth and open-air. As I walk in, I realise that something has changed. The teak table is scored with knife marks, the drawers of the oak desk have been flung to the floor. In the chief reception room with the full-length windows and the cord-waisted velvet curtains, there's an intruder with his mind on ransom. Cowboy, not hesitating, jumps him and knocks him smack on the floor.

When he has been led away, it's Cowboy, not me, gets the attention. And it was all, I know, on my account.

Your shoulders, Cowboy, and your rustic croon
have become welcome to me.
Sinking on you is as good
as a lie-down in a meadow
or a walk beside the long acre
with its crop of small suns and full moons.

I turn to you when the going gets rough,
when friends are vague or complex.
I find in your raspish chin and thickened fingers
something softer than clean,
finer than carpets,
never itching the nose.
There are random blue specks on your skin
that remind me you've been places,
you've smelt down and fur, hoof and hair.
You've pulled calves from puzzled cows
and there's something you know about me
that sofas don't.

This Awkward Love

This awkward love is what the family confers,
so children are held in comfort and I responsible,
one man my guard against all the rest.

It puzzles me
how others bask in the Sunday dinner code,
as if any attempt at symmetry
will provide foundation.

Who am I to say,
who have always wanted everything,
that this is right or not?
Society is a bearable construct.
Pick your meaning.

No, says the earthy West Cork girl,
it's not enough to be friends
But neither she nor my feminist acquaintance
will come between the sheets,
tell me I'm great and be family.

This awkward love
may be a kind of reverence for history.
One night in a dream I saw this:
I'm a tribeswoman in ceremonial dress
and I sit as if others must stand.
He comes to me with sweat on his hands
and a childlike question in wounded eyes.
He has failed to kill the bear. Will I still accept him?
My white skirt spreads like a wedding train.
I give no answer.

THE LAST LIFE PERHAPS DEPARTING

The bullhead rises and closes in.
Here come my past lives.
I see myself pinned against a wall,
then fallen on the streets of Pamplona
with my stomach open.
Again, crouching with Mexican women
in a dank prison,
until the warder lets in a chink of fatal light.
Moves a stiletto towards my eye.

And now the devil I don't believe in
struts towards me like a master.
His red-teethed hounds attend,
eyes on honey-glaze.
I would be theirs,
but some lighter being lifts me,
hands under my armpits, like a baby.

She says:
'You have me at your back, my dear.
I can take you to your cubby,
to the peace they can't ruffle,
where the couching air welcomes,
grass waves without break
and watching mountains hide no fire'.

The mourners have stayed for two days.
The house is black with them.
I'm to-ing and fro-ing with funeral fare,
my head an earthenware jar.

Sunday evening comes.
The crowd genies down to
my brother and sister and their earnest faces.
You know what, I say,
I can't remember the funeral or the mass.
I should remember the bells
and some movement of people
to and from the pulpit.
And how could the burial be wiped out?
How could I forget the first thud of earth,
that she always said was the shutting door,
the final plutonic hello?

Look, he says, when people go crazed
it can be kindness to calm them.
You wouldn't want to go off the rails, overboard.
You drugged me?
I turn to my sister. She looks down and away.
You drugged me?

There's that sound that has no sense,
a clotted swell like the tail-end of a hurricane,
a voiceless laugh because the world is pulling out,
nothing in it but me, and then how am I to
understand?
In the end was no word.
I don't ever again, I say, ever again,
want to be drugged without my knowledge.

I'm a bully,
ranting at the wrong people as usual.
The noise burgeons and I pin it somewhere
in the lower rear of my cerebellum.
My head is a private stereo –
walls of sound.
Prison gets you everywhere.

Though my eyes can't function,
I know the others have slipped from the room
and are already beyond the limits.

GEMINI

EXACTING

Mirroring is never exact.
The chrome of the bath-taps
tarnishes in the water
and the yellow shampoo bottle
turns dull cream.

Take the autumn picture –
trees pinnacled in orange
at this, the time of their decline.
If you painted
you would probably give them a reflection,
as if the trees liked to be mimicked by water,
though it can't give roundness to the bark,
smell to the resin, sound to the touching of leaves;
nor the special dimension
in the inevitable progress of brown.

I wait here whipped by sudden storms,
in the hope that sometime I'll look in the water
and from it will emerge a four-dimensional replica,
who will tell me by her knobbled bark,
her inner movements and her servitude to time,
how my sap rises,
why I lean this way and not the other,
why my seeds are beyond my control.

But water is as much in flux as I am,
and so are you, in whom I have looked for my face.

CON

You told yourself passion would guide you;
no ordinary life would grab
and stick you in a built-in wardrobe,
perch you on a wooden hanger.
You denied the conscious effort,
thought the clay could be slapped on
without attention,
though the wheel careered at top speed.

You've made a mess and ended with a crooked vessel
you can't put flowers in or pour milk from.
Maybe it will do for watering if you ever sow.

You lash into your capsule, he into his.
Full speed incommunicado in the same orbit.
Can't decide who's the satellite and who the mover,
and neither is prime anyhow.
What you've chosen, by default,
is a home as silent as your first,
a set of tasks lonely, futile and abandoned.
The negation of a thing you wished to have
and a punishment
created easily in one reflexive con.

underneath blankets and someone
agrees with your pleasure principle
pampers your stomach with baby kisses
your pink parts sucked and singing
better in the dark
where you couldn't look down
and see your legs not pfeiffer's
more like badly mashed spuds
crinkling at the horizon
or where the mattress spreads them
better not seeing his face to remember
your eyes don't meet they avoid
better not having to think again
how distant you are
and not the yoke and white
except of a too thinly fried egg
let your skin think for itself
that in another age you wouldn't wish
for any more than a good man who'd stroke you
who'd bring back the kill which you'd gut and garnish
could do worse than this
then the blankets are off
and doing it doggy style
your stomach goes like someone took a fork
and finished off the look of a heap of mash
the skin runs from side to side
like a manic patch of sea
you try to adopt a position that stops it
wonder if a little more callanetics
would make you taut
wonder if he minds the spud look
he is so patriotic
and it is because you bore the children
fluid with maternal solicitude

could do worse than this
except when the push is on
you remember those lesbians you refused
who cackle in your lost opportunity space
when it comes to the skin everything is an affair

Media

What you hear
on the propagation of a flower,
the second law of thermodynamics,
Fermat's last theorem
and a scroll of other matters
will stay or not –
depending on your current need
and whether the facts find an echo
among the snagging ancient feelers
on the bottom of your personal,
ever-shifting riverbed.

Here's the information attack.
Always has been status attack.
Wish I lived in Chaucer's time,
when I might have read all the books.
Now a book is a piece of airborne dust,
instantly replaced once whooshed.

Who do you wear?
How do you hang your hat?
From a thousand choose one,
or stand stony on the shore
with the wide indexed tide rolling in.

X has sold a million books.
Y has sold two.
A B and C are such good writers
they got 500,000 each and that's just an advance.
Mary has a business worth a bomb.
Sylvie's one of the richest women in Ireland.
There's another self-made man.
I've definitely failed.

The odd time I soak myself in silence.
No thought,
only mechanical domestic acts
or the eating of a meal.
Those moments of no epiphany.
Or of some sudden decision you'll always remember.
And you were only looking out the window
at the unremarkable, could say barren, garden.

When I close my eyes
I see a white figure on a mountain path,
the mist of a medieval painting her destination.
Has she read
Doestoevskypushkinmolieredickensrussellgarcialorca
pablonerudaczeslawmiloszgertrudesteinhildadoolittle
sheridanlefanuelizabethbishopwilliamtrevorflannobrie
njohnbanvillerichardellmangerardmanleyhopkinscarlj
ungpatrickmccabekateobrienannemccaffreyisobelallen
de?
Does she have
an MAMSCMPHILPHDHDTVSUV,
wear
Guccipradaivesstlaurentjimmychoolouisvuitton;
and if not,
what's she worth?

Three

There's one thing you wish for at three,
when an army has invaded your forehead
and the rain has something against
the clothes you've hung on the line
and forgotten to bring in –
and that's certainty.

At three it would ease
to feel a big hand smooth down your nose,
sweeten to own a pet John Travolta,
who would dimple just for you
and tell you something slow.

Some people enjoy their lives,
you know it's true.
They eat dinner unrushed,
the fork like a mother's feeding hand
leaving *I love you* on the tongue.

Might be that disgruntled e-message
and the clamour of silent voices queued to be read
that shook the shoulder this time.

Or else it's him, home from the Hill of Laurels,
which is forever in erosion,
threatening to be sucked
by a force stronger than all of us.
And his constant watchful pose –
no space for anything small
or a moment of inattention to the goal,
such as:
I hate this way of life. I nearly walked out today I felt such a waste.

Then there's the work you've been lax about
and the ocean of PhDs who've got it made
and the bleak shocks of your mind's embedded
symbiont
to shake you wide alone.

'An Ordinary Lane' was published in *Poetry Ireland Review,* Autumn 1998. 'Dream of a Yellow Wolf' appeared in *Honest Ulsterman – Autumn Journals,* September 1998. 'Last', 'Big Bong' and 'Dream of a Yellow Wolf' were included in *When the Air Inhales You* (Arlen House, 2008). 'Lesson' was published in *Verse – Women Irish Poets,* Volume 16, Number 2, 1999. 'Medicine' appeared in Louise C. Callaghan (ed), *Forgotten Light* (A. & A. Farmar, 2003).

The following poems are on the CD, *Out of My Skin* (Odin Poetries, 2002): 'The Emerald Pool', 'Nick Cave Makes Love to Me', 'China', 'Saturday Morning'.

ABOUT THE AUTHOR

Máighréad Medbh was born in Newcastle West, County Limerick. She has published four previous poetry collections: *The Making of a Pagan* (Blackstaff Press, 1990); *Tenant* (Salmon Publishing, 1999); *Split* (in *¡Divas!*, Arlen House, 2003); and *When the Air Inhales You* (Arlen House, 2008). She produced a CD, *Out of My Skin*, in 2002, and her work has been included in a wide range of anthologies and journals.

Máighréad has become widely known as a powerful and affecting performance poet. She has appeared at a large number of venues in Ireland, Great Britain, the United States, mainland Europe and on the broadcast media. She has finished the first in a four-volume fantasy for children and is currently writing a non-fiction book on the subject of solitude.

Máighréad is on the web at: www.maighreadmedbh.ie